Silly Sketcher

Draw Puns!

written by Luke Colins

illustrated by Catherine Cates

BLACK RABBIT BOOKS

Hi Jinx is published by Black Rabbit Books
P.O. Box 3263, Mankato, Minnesota, 56002.
www.blackrabbitbooks.com

Jennifer Besel, editor; Michael Sellner and Catherine Cates, designers; Omay Ayres, photo researcher

Library of Congress Cataloging-in-Publication Data
Names: Colins, Luke, author.
Title: Draw puns! / by Luke Colins.
Description: Mankato, Minnesota : Black Rabbit Books, 2019. | Series: Hi jinx. Silly sketcher | Includes bibliographical references and index. | Audience: Ages 8-12, | Audience: Grades 4 to 6.
Identifiers: LCCN 2018000412 (print) | LCCN 2018005914 (ebook) | ISBN 9781680726060 (e-book) | ISBN 9781680726008 (library binding) | ISBN 9781680727487 (pbk.)
Subjects: LCSH: Cartooning—Technique—Juvenile literature. | Plays on words—Juvenile literature.
Classification: LCC NC1764 (ebook) | LCC NC1764 .C655 2019 (print) | DDC 741.5/1—dc23
LC record available at https://lccn.loc.gov/2018000412

Printed in the United States. 4/18

Image Credits

Alamy: Matthew Cole, 2–3, 5 (markers); iStock: carbouval, 5 (pencil sharpener & eraser); Shutterstock: designer_an, 19 (waves bkgd); Mario Pantelic, Cover, Back Cover, 3, 5, 12 (line doodle bkgd); Memo Angeles, Cover (kids), 4 (boy & dog), 5 (kids & sign), 6 (girl), 8 (girl & pencil), 10 (girl), 12 (girl), 14 (boy), 17 (animals), 20 (all), 23 (girl); Olga Sabo, 5 (colored pencils); opicobello, 7 (torn paper), 13 (marker strokes), 19 (torn paper); owatta, 5 (paper); Pasko Maksim, Back Cover, 11, 23, 24 (torn paper); Pitju, 3, 9, 15, 21 (curled corner); Ron Dale, 3–7, 11, 13, 19, 20 (marker stroke), totallypic, 4 (arrow) Every effort has been made to contact copyright holders for material reproduced in this book. Any omissions will be rectified in subsequent printings if notice is given to the publisher.

Contents

Chapter 1
Be a Silly Sketcher!

Drawing is fun. But drawing puns is **hilarious**! Not sure what a pun is? A pun is a joke that plays with words that sound similar. Puns can also play with different meanings of words or phrases.

To be a punny sketcher, all you need is a pencil, some paper, and a funny bone. Just follow the steps. You'll have everyone laughing with your drawings in no time.

What You Need

Chapter 2

Put Your Pencil to the Paper

Kids are great at "rolling their eyes." Turn that phrase into a pun with this silly sketch.

Step 1

Start the eyes by drawing two large circles. Draw smaller circles inside the first ones. Then add **pupils** inside those circles.

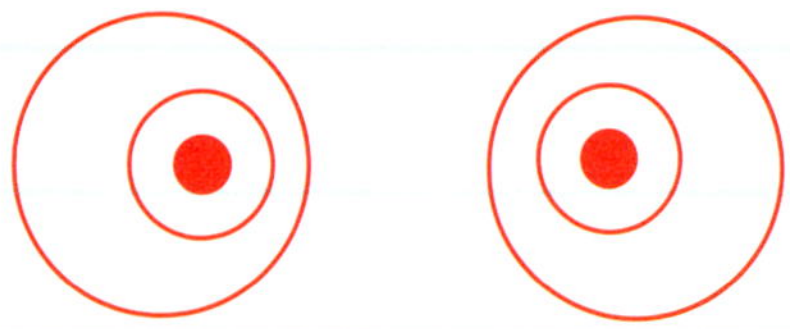

Step 2

Add mouths inside each large circle. Add eyelashes too.

Step 3

Use straight lines to make arms and legs. Use dots for knees and hands.

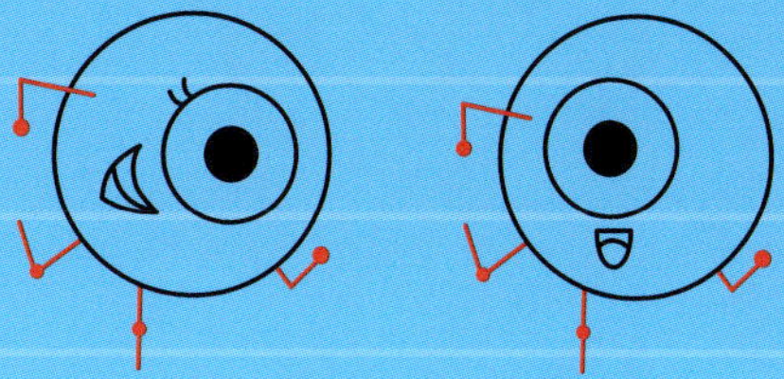

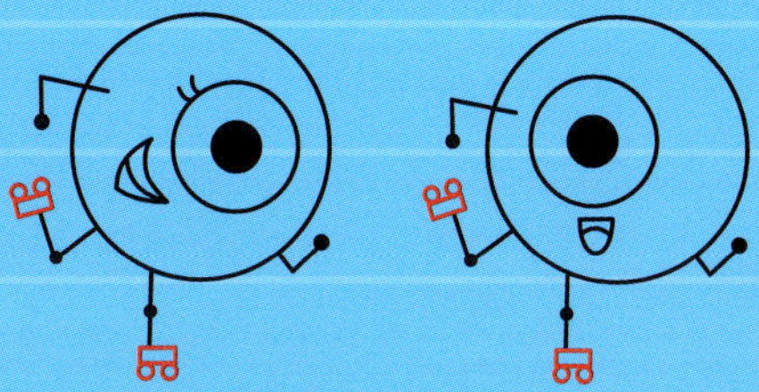

Step 4

Make your eyes roll with roller skates.

Step 5

Add some fun **motion** lines.

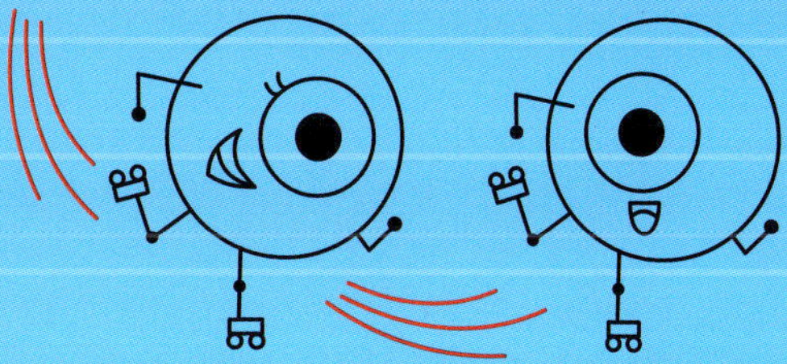

Finish It Up!

Use markers to **outline** your drawing. Then try colored pencils for shading it in.

Wandering Mind

Where does your mind go when it wanders?

Step 1
Start with two circles. Then draw a squiggly line in the shape of a brain.

Step 2
Use straight lines to make arms and legs. Use dots for knees.

Step 3

Add eyebrows and details to the eyes.

Step 4

Erase the **overlapping** lines inside the shapes.

Step 5

Add a mouth.

Step 6

Add detail lines to your wandering mind.

The Keys to Happiness

Maybe the keys to happiness are on your keyboard!

Step 1

Draw two small rectangles. Put **punctuation** marks inside them.

Step 2

Make the rectangles look like 3-D computer keys.

Step 3

Add two circles to each key to start the eyes.

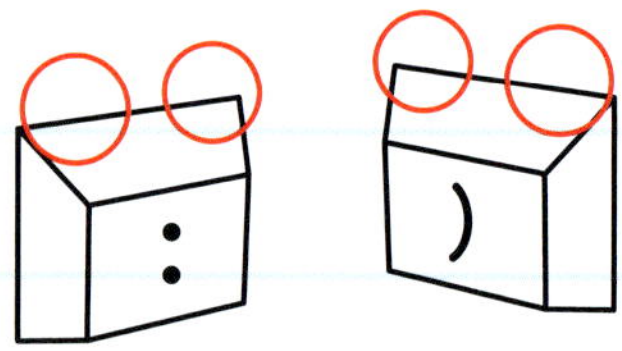

Tip Try adding a background to the sketch. Maybe show the keys jumping off a keyboard.

Step 4

Erase the overlapping lines inside the shapes.

Step 5

Add face details, such as funny eyebrows and laughing mouths.

Step 6

Use curved lines to make arms and hands.

Step 7

Give the keys bent legs.

Step 8

Add motion lines to make the keys jump.

Spring Chicken

Some adults call young people "spring chickens." A chicken on a spring isn't what they mean. But it's sure fun to draw!

Step 1
Draw a big swirled line.

Step 2
Add two large circles. Use triangles for a beak.

Step 3
Erase the overlapping lines inside the shapes.

Step 4

Give your chicken a comb and **wattle**. Add eye and beak details too.

Step 5

Draw funny wings off the sides of the spring.

Step 6

Add some silly feet too.

Step 7

Show the chicken's wild bouncing with motion lines.

Finish It Up!

Color your spring chicken however you'd like. Maybe it would be funnier with purple wings.

Home Run

Turn the baseball phrase "home run" into a silly pun.

Step 1

Start the house by drawing a rectangle. Add two lines off one end.

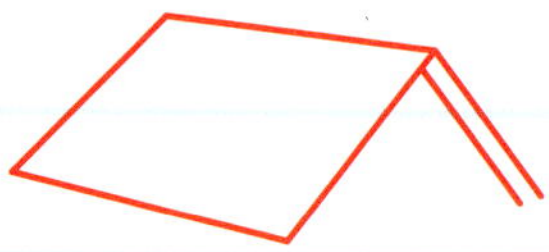

Step 2

Use straight lines to make walls and a window.

Step 3

Use circles and curved lines to start a face.

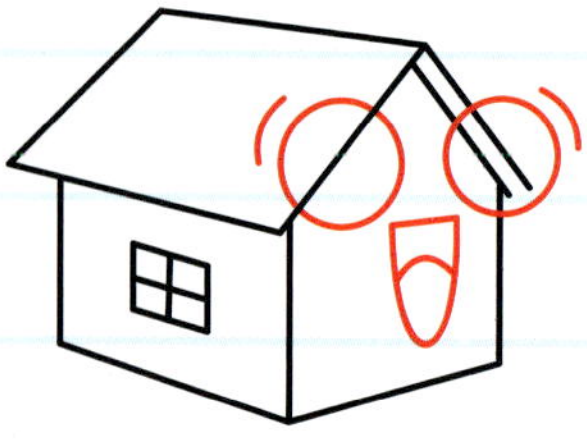

Step 4

Erase the overlapping lines inside the shapes.

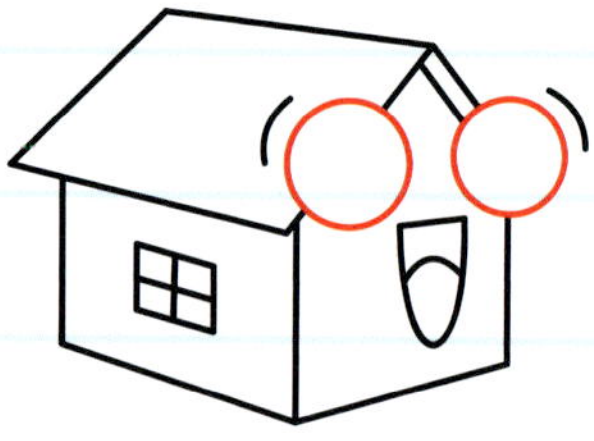

Step 5

Add details, such as arms and eyebrows.

Step 6

Give your home legs and a chimney.

Step 7

Draw smoke from the chimney. Add motion lines to show your home run.

No Bear Feet!

This pun makes spelling funny! Bare feet don't have any shoes. Bear feet belong to the hairy forest animal.

Step 1

Draw a balloon shape for a head. Then add a skinny body and legs.

Step 2

Start the eyes with big circles. Add arms too.

Step 3

Add the outline of the person's hair. Draw a signpost too.

Step 4

Use squiggly lines to start furry feet on the person. Draw grass and a sign on the signpost.

Step 5

Add detail to make the sign look 3-D. Give the person's bear feet some toes.

Step 6

Erase all the overlapping lines inside the shapes.

Step 7

Add details, such as claws, to the person.

Step 8

Give the person face details. Write a message on the sign.

Remote Island

The word remote has several meanings. It can mean far away. It can also be the thing that turns on the TV.

Step 1

Start by drawing a **lopsided** oval. Put a square inside the oval.

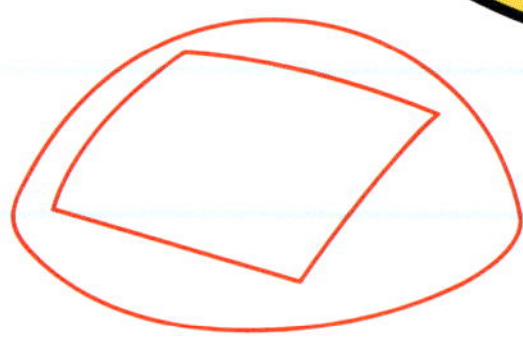

Step 2

Draw two rectangle boxes inside the square. Start the trunk of a tree too.

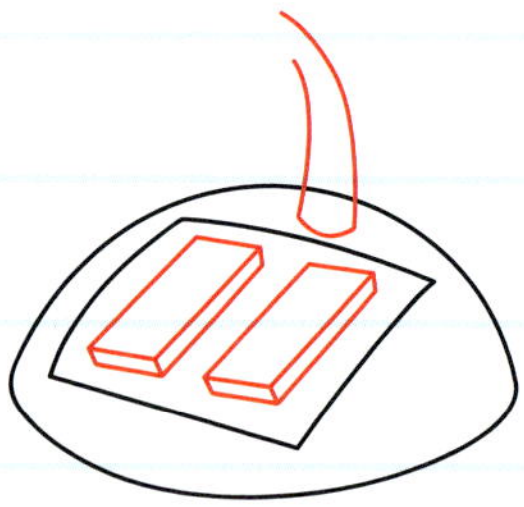

Step 3

Give the tree leaves. Add sunglasses and smiles to the rectangles.

Step 4

Draw two small circles in the tree's leaves. Give one rectangle a book.

Step 5

Erase all the overlapping lines inside the shapes.

Step 6

Add buttons to the rectangles to make them look like remote controls.

Step 7

Draw funny arms and legs coming off the remotes.

Step 8

Add detail lines to your drawing.

Tip Try adding an ocean background to your picture.

Chapter 3

Get in on the Hi Jinx

Graphic artists use the same steps you just did! They use simple shapes to build the frames of their drawings. Sometimes they use puns to add humor. Maybe you'll draw a comic book one day.

Take It One Step More

1. Does drawing puns make them more or less humorous?

2. Are your sketches more or less funny with color? Why?

3. Why is it important to erase overlapping lines?

GLOSSARY

hilarious (hih-LAR-ee-uhs)—very funny

lopsided (LAHP-sy-did)—uneven on one side

motion (MO-shun)—an act or process of moving

outline (AHWT-lyn)—to draw a line around the edges of something

overlap (oh-vur-LAP)—to extend over or past

punctuation (punk-shoo-AY-shun)—marks that are written to clarify the meaning of a sentence, such as a period or comma

pupil (PYU-pul)—the part of the eye that lets light in; in people, it's the round, black part of the eye.

wattle (WAH-tuhl)—a fleshy part usually around the head or neck of a bird

LEARN MORE

BOOKS

Antram, David. *Caricatures.* Step-by-Step Draw. Mankato, MN: Book House, 2017.

Beaumont, Steve. *How to Draw Weird Fantasy Art.* Creating Fantasy Art. New York: Rosen, 2018.

Johnson, Clare. *How to Draw.* New York: Dorling Kindersley Limited, 2017.

WEBSITES

Drawing for Kids
mocomi.com/fun/arts-crafts/drawing-for-kids/

Drawing for Kids
www.hellokids.com/r_12/drawing-for-kids/

How to Draw for Kids
www.artforkidshub.com/how-to-draw/

TIPS AND TRICKS

Make sure to let the marker outlines dry before coloring in your drawings.

Colored pencils are a great tool for coloring in your drawings. Layer one color over another for a cool blended effect.

Can't draw a straight line? Try using a ruler or other straight edge.

Don't worry if your drawings don't look exactly like the ones in this book! Art is all about creating your own thing. Just have fun!